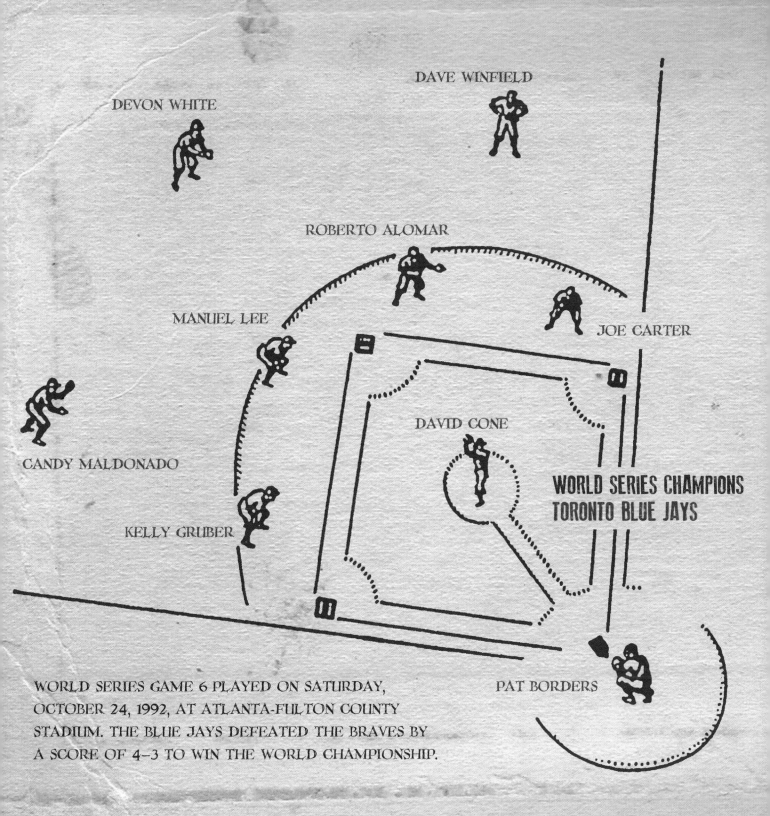

DAVE WINFIELD

DEVON WHITE

ROBERTO ALOMAR

MANUEL LEE

JOE CARTER

CANDY MALDONADO

DAVID CONE

WORLD SERIES CHAMPIONS
TORONTO BLUE JAYS

KELLY GRUBER

PAT BORDERS

WORLD SERIES GAME 6 PLAYED ON SATURDAY,
OCTOBER 24, 1992, AT ATLANTA-FULTON COUNTY
STADIUM. THE BLUE JAYS DEFEATED THE BRAVES BY
A SCORE OF 4–3 TO WIN THE WORLD CHAMPIONSHIP.

WORLD SERIES CHAMPIONS

TORONTO BLUE JAYS

SARA GILBERT

CREATIVE EDUCATION

Published by Creative Education
P.O. Box 227, Mankato, Minnesota 56002
Creative Education is an imprint of The Creative Company
www.thecreativecompany.us

Design and production by Blue Design (www.bluedes.com)
Art direction by Rita Marshall
Printed in the United States of America

Photographs by Getty Images (Abelimages, Bernstein Associates,
Lisa Blumenfeld, John Capella/Sports Imagery, Jonaathan Daniel/
Allsport, Diamond Images, Otto Greule Jr., Otto Greule/Allsport,
Tom G. Lynn/Time & Life Pictures, Brad Mangin/MLB Photos, Jim
McIsaac, MLB Photos, Redroom Studios, John Reid/MLB Photos,
John Reid III/MLB Photos, Chris Ruppmann/NY Daily News
Archive, Dave Sandford, Rob Skeoch/MLB Photos, Larry W. Smith,
Chuck Solomon/Sports Illustrated, Rick Stewart, Rick Stewart/
Allsport, George Tiedemann/Sports Illustrated, Ron Vesely/MLB
Photos)

Library of Congress Cataloging-in-Publication Data
Gilbert, Sara.
Toronto Blue Jays / Sara Gilbert.
p. cm. — (World series champions)
Includes bibliographical references and index.
Summary: A simple introduction to the Toronto Blue Jays major
league baseball team, including its start in 1977, its World Series
triumphs, and its stars throughout the years.
ISBN 978-1-60818-273-2
1. Toronto Blue Jays (Baseball team)—History—Juvenile literature.
I. Title.
GV875.T67G55 2013
796.357'6409713541—dc23   2012004267

First edition
9 8 7 6 5 4 3 2 1

Cover: Right fielder José Bautista
Page 2: Right fielder Edwin Encarnacion
Page 3: Pitcher Jimmy Key
Right: Blue Jays in the 1993 World Series

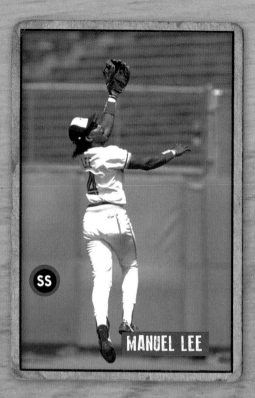

SS

MANUEL LEE

3B

PAUL MOLITOR

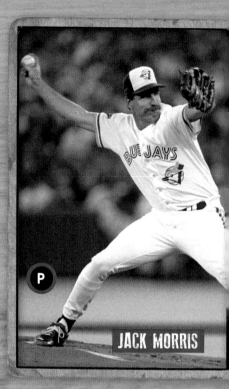

P

JACK MORRIS

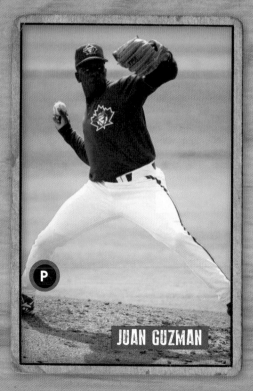

P

JUAN GUZMAN

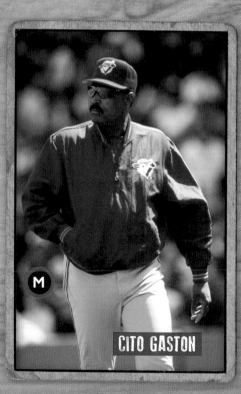

M

CITO GASTON

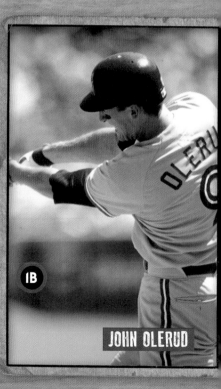

1B

JOHN OLERUD

TABLE OF CONTENTS

TORONTO BLUE JAYS

TORONTO AND ROGERS CENTRE

Toronto is a city in the Canadian **PROVINCE** of Ontario. With 2.5 million people, it is the biggest city in Canada. Toronto has a stadium named Rogers Centre. A baseball team called the Blue Jays plays there.

RIVALS AND COLORS

The Blue Jays are 1 of 30 teams in Major League Baseball. All the major-league teams try to win the World Series and become world champions. The Blue Jays wear black, blue, white, and gray uniforms. They are **RIVALS** of the Boston Red Sox.

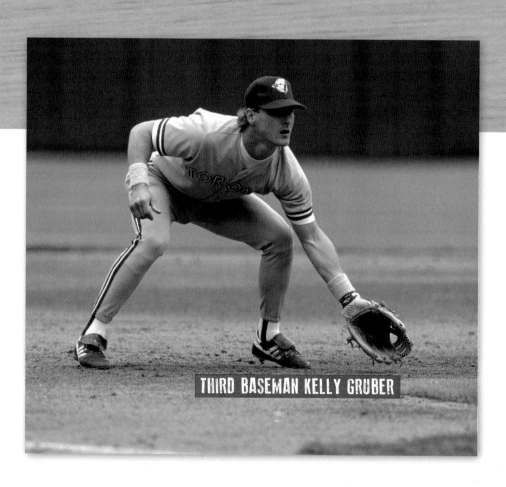

THIRD BASEMAN KELLY GRUBER

RIGHT FIELDER DAVE WINFIELD

BLUE JAYS HISTORY

The Blue Jays played their first season in 1977. It snowed during their first game, but the fans warmed up when the Blue Jays won! For several years, the Blue Jays lost more games than they won.

A 1977 BLUE JAYS GAME

C

PAT BORDERS

2B

AARON HILL

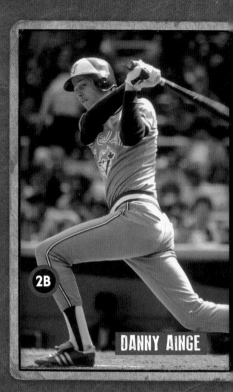

2B

DANNY AINGE

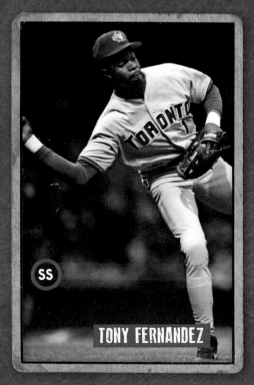

SS

TONY FERNANDEZ

CF

VERNON WELLS

LF

GEORGE BELL

DAVE STIEB

In 1983, Toronto started winning more often. In 1985 and 1989, strong-armed pitcher Dave Stieb helped the Blue Jays make it to the **PLAYOFFS**. But they lost before the World Series both times.

CARLOS DELGADO

Manager Cito Gaston led the Blue Jays to victory in the 1992 World Series. VERSATILE second baseman Roberto Alomar helped Toronto win the world championship again the very next year!

Strong first baseman Carlos Delgado bashed 336 home runs for the Blue Jays. He helped Toronto win a lot of games. But they were not able to get back to the playoffs again.

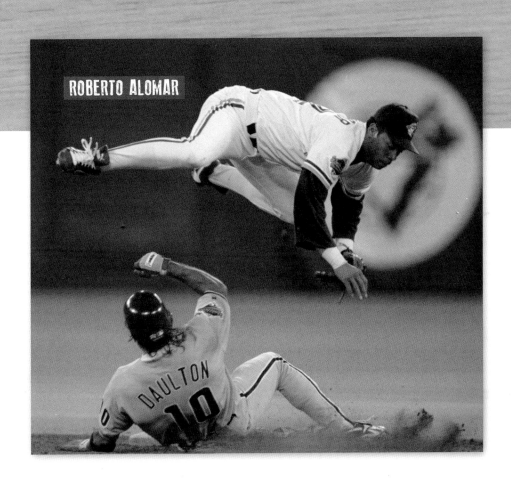

ROBERTO ALOMAR

ALFREDO GRIFFIN

JOE CARTER

BLUE JAYS STARS

In 1979, young shortstop Alfredo Griffin won the **ROOKIE** of the Year award. He was a fast runner. In 1983, powerful center fielder Lloyd Moseby scored more than 100 runs for the Blue Jays.

Outfielder Joe Carter came to Toronto in 1990. He hit the winning home run in the 1993 World Series. In 2003, pitcher Roy

Halladay won 22 games for the Blue Jays. He got an award as the best pitcher in the league.

In 2009, the Blue Jays added outfielder José Bautista. He slugged 54 home runs in 2010. That was more homers than any other player in baseball hit that season. Fans hoped Bautista's powerful swing would push the Blue Jays to another world championship soon!

JOSÉ BAUTISTA

ROY HALLADAY

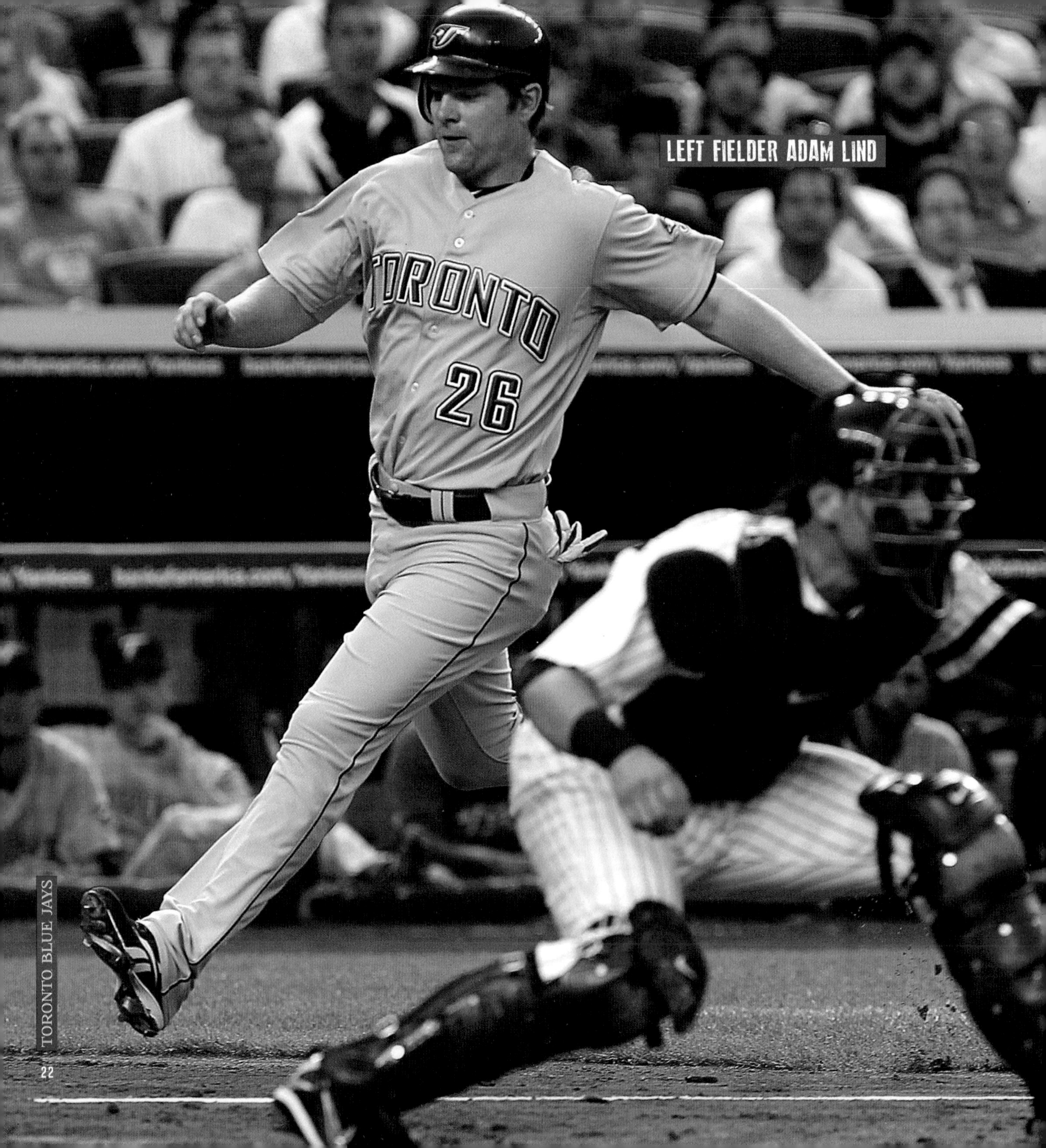

LEFT FIELDER ADAM LIND

HOW THE BLUE JAYS GOT THEIR NAME

The Blue Jays were named by their fans. The owners of the team asked people to send in ideas for the team name. Fans sent more than 4,000 ideas. The owners thought the best name was the Blue Jays, which are loud, blue birds.

ABOUT THE BLUE JAYS

First season: 1977

League/division: American League, East Division

World Series championships:

1992   *4 games to 2 versus Atlanta Braves*

1993   *4 games to 2 versus Philadelphia Phillies*

Blue Jays Web site for kids:

http://mlb.mlb.com/tor/fan_forum/kids_index.jsp

Club MLB:

http://web.clubmlb.com/index.html

GLOSSARY

PLAYOFFS — all the games (including the World Series) after the regular season that are played to decide who the champion will be

PROVINCE — a certain area of land within a country, like a state

RIVALS — teams that play extra hard against each other

ROOKIE — an athlete playing his or her first year

VERSATILE — able to do many different things well

INDEX